DISCARD

```
F
1608     Evans
.E92       The Caribbean
1973       (the English-speaking
           islands) in pictures
```

7460430

The CARIBBEAN
(The ENGLISH-SPEAKING ISLANDS)
in pictures

VISUAL
GEOGRAPHY
SERIES

A donkey cart is a means of transportation for this lady in rural Barbados.

Prepared by LANCELOT O. EVANS

STERLING PUBLISHING CO., INC. NEW YORK

Oak Tree Press Co., Ltd.
London & Sydney

VISUAL GEOGRAPHY SERIES

Afghanistan	Denmark	Iceland	Malaysia and Singapore	Scotland
Alaska	Ecuador	India	Mexico	South Africa
Argentina	Egypt	Indonesia	Morocco	Spain
Australia	England	Iran	Nepal	Surinam
Austria	Ethiopia	Iraq	New Zealand	Sweden
Belgium and Luxembourg	Fiji	Ireland	Norway	Switzerland
Berlin—East and West	Finland	Islands of the Mediterranean	Pakistan and Bangladesh	Tahiti and the French Islands of the Pacific
Brazil	France	Israel	Panama and the Canal Zone	
Bulgaria	French Canada	Italy	Peru	Taiwan
Canada	Ghana	Jamaica	The Philippines	Tanzania
The Caribbean (English-Speaking Islands)	Greece	Japan	Poland	Thailand
Ceylon (Sri Lanka)	Greenland	Kenya	Portugal	Tunisia
Chile	Guatemala	Korea	Puerto Rico	Turkey
China	Hawaii	Kuwait	Rhodesia	Venezuela
Colombia	Holland	Lebanon	Rumania	Wales
Cuba	Honduras	Liberia	Russia	West Germany
Czechoslovakia	Hong Kong	Malawi	Saudi Arabia	Yugoslavia
	Hungary			

A dolphin and his trainer put on a show for visitors to Nassau's Seafloor Aquarium, where hundreds of marine creatures found in Bahamian waters, including giant turtles and exotic fish, are on view.

PICTURE CREDITS

The publishers wish to thank the following for the use of the photographs in this book: ALCOA Steamship Co.; Bahamas Development Board; Bahamas Ministry of Tourism; Bahamas News Bureau; Barbados Publicity Committee, New York; Barbados Tourist Board, New York; British Information Services, London; British Overseas Airways Corporation; KLM Royal Dutch Airlines; Museum of the American Indian, Heye Foundation; National Aeronautics and Space Administration, Washington; Qantas Airlines; Royal Mail Lines, Ltd.; Taylor Woodrow Group, Southall, England; Trinidad and Tobago Tourist Board; United Nations, New York; United States Virgin Islands Government; West India Committee, London.

Seventh Printing, 1973
Copyright © 1973, 1971, 1969, 1968 by Sterling Publishing Co., Inc.
419 Park Avenue South, New York, N.Y. 10016
British edition published by Oak Tree Press Co., Ltd., Nassau, Bahamas
Distributed in Australia and New Zealand by Oak Tree Press Co., Ltd.,
P.O. Box 34, Brickfield Hill, Sydney 2000, N.S.W.
Distributed in the United Kingdom and elsewhere in the British Commonwealth
by Ward Lock Ltd., 116 Baker Street, London W 1
Manufactured in the United States of America   All rights reserved
Library of Congress Catalog Card No.: 68-18795
ISBN 0-8069-1096-8   UK 7061-2121-X
1097-6

CONTENTS

INTRODUCTION 5
HISTORY 7
THE BAHAMAS AND THE NORTHERN ISLANDS ... 11
THE VIRGIN ISLANDS 28
BARBADOS AND THE ENGLISH-SPEAKING
  ISLANDS OF THE EASTERN CARIBBEAN 35
TRINIDAD AND TOBAGO 51

INDEX

Abercrombie, Ralph, 52
Adams, Grantley, 37
Africans, 9
AGRICULTURE, 56
Andros Island, 14
ANGUILLA, 8, 32, 37, 39, 41, 44, 45, 49
ANTIGUA, 6, 8, 9, 32, 37, 39–41, 43, 44, 49
Antilles, Greater, 5, 9
Antilles, Lesser, 5, 6, 9, 35, 42
Apollo 9 astronauts, 25
Arawaks, 6, 8, 9, 30, 51
Ardastra Gardens, 24
ART, MUSIC AND CARNIVAL, 58–60
Asphalt, 55, 56
BAHAMAS AND OTHER NORTHERN ISLANDS, 5–8, 11–27
BARBADOS AND THE ENGLISH-SPEAKING ISLANDS OF THE CARIBBEAN, 6–9, 35–49, 61
Barbados Labour Party, 37
Barbuda, 8, 41
Barrow, Earl F., 37
"Bearded," 35
Bermuda, 8, 27
Bimini, 12, 14, 20, 21
Bird of Paradise Island, 55
Bridgetown, 35, 39, 40, 45
Britain, 8, 9, 11, 32, 39, 40, 52
BRITISH VIRGIN ISLANDS, 31–33
Calypso, 59
Campos, Pedro, 8, 35
Caribs, 6, 8, 9, 11, 30, 51
Carnival, 28
CARONI, 62
Caroni River, 51
CAYMAN ISLANDS, 6, 23, 24
Charles I, King, 11
Charles II, King, 11
Charlotte Amalie, 28, 30
Charlotteville, 55
Chinese, 9
Christiansted, 30
Civil War, American, 12
CLIMATE
  Bahamas, 14
  Trinidad-Tobago, 55
  Virgin Islands, British, 32
  Virgin Islands, U.S., 30
Cocoa, 51, 56, 62, 63
"Coconut water," 63
Codrington College, 48
Columbus, Christopher, 7, 8, 11, 15, 23, 28, 32, 35, 44, 51
Constantine, Learie, 53
Constitution of 1964, 14
Coral Bay, 28
Crafts, 20, 23
CROWN COLONY STATUS, 52, 53
Cruz Bay, 28
Cuba, 5, 7, 11
Democratic Labour Party, 37

Democratic League, 36, 37
Denmark, 28
Devil's Woodyard, 62
Diseases, 30
DOMINICA, 6–9, 37, 39, 40–42, 45, 49
East Indians, 52, 57, 59, 61
East Indies, 7
ECONOMY
  Bahamas, 18–23
  Barbados, 45–49
  Trinidad-Tobago, 55–57
  Virgin Islands, British, 33
  Virgin Islands, U.S., 30
EDUCATION, 60, 61
Eleuthera, 11–13, 17, 21, 23, 25
Emancipation of Slaves Bill, 52, 59
ENGLISH, 52, 53
Exuma, 12, 20, 21
FEDERATION, 37, 38, 44, 54
Fort Charlotte, 25
France, 8
Freeport, 14, 21
Fyzabad, 63
GEOGRAPHICAL DIVISIONS,
  Trinidad-Tobago, 62–64
GEOGRAPHY
  Bahamas, 12–14
  Barbados, 40–42
  Virgin Islands, 29, 30
Georgetown, 24
GOVERNMENT
  Bahamas, 14–16
  Barbados, 36
  Trinidad-Tobago, 54
  Virgin Islands, British, 33
  Virgin Islands, U.S., 31
Government House, 15
Governor
  Bahamas, 14
  Virgin Islands, U.S., 30
Governor General, Barbados, 36
Grand Bahama, 12–14, 21
GRENADA, 6, 9, 37, 39, 41–45
Haiti, 11
Hamilton, Alexander, 29, 44
Harvey, Admiral, 52
Hemingway, Ernest, 20
Hindu, 9, 58, 59
Hispaniola, 5, 7
HISTORY, 7–9
  Barbados, 35, 36
  Virgin Islands, British, 32
House of Assembly
  Bahamas, 14–16
  Barbados, 36
  Virgin Islands, British, 32
"Iere," 51
Indentured workers, 9, 52
INDEPENDENCE, 35, 38, 54
Indians, 9
INDUSTRIAL DEVELOPMENT, 56, 57
INTRODUCTION, 5, 6

Jamaica, 5, 7, 23, 27, 38, 53, 61
James I, King, 35
La Brea, 55, 56, 63
Lagoon Bouff, 62
Las Virgines, 32
Leeward Islands, 7, 32, 35, 38, 40
Legislative Building, 38
Legislative Council, 32
Limbo dance, 63
"Los Barbados," see "Bearded"
MAYARO, 62
Montserrat, 8, 32, 34, 39–41, 44, 49
"Mother Colony of the West Indies," 44
Mountains
  Boggy Peak, 44
  Grand Piton, 45
  Morne Diablotin, 42
  Morne Garu, 45
  Mount Misery, 44
  Mt. St. Catherine, 42
  Nevis Peak, 44
  Petit Piton, 45
  Soufrière, 45
Muslims, 58–60
NARIVA, 62
Nassau, 11–13, 15, 18
Nelson, Admiral, 43
Nelson's Dockyard, 40
NEVIS, 8, 37, 39, 41, 44
NEW CONSTITUTION, 53
New Plymouth Town, 15
New Providence, 12, 13, 18
Oil, 21, 55, 56, 62, 63
O'Neale, Charles, 37
Organic Act of 1954, 31
Organization of American States, 37, 54
THE PEOPLE, 57–60
PEOPLE'S NATIONAL MOVEMENT, 53, 54
Pindling, Lynden, 16
Pitch Lake, 56, 63
Plantation Fort, 35
Plantations, 21, 36
Ponce de Leon, 27
POPULATION
  Bahamas, 18
  Barbados, 40–42
  Virgin Islands, British, 33
Port of Spain, 51, 52, 58, 60, 61, 63
Portugal, 8
Premier, Bahamas, 17
Prime Minister, Barbados, 36, 37
Puerto Rico, 6, 7
Queen Elizabeth II Hospital, 47
"Red House," 52
Redonda, 41
RELIGION, 16
Rogers, Woodes, 11
Royal Cedula, 52
Ruiz de Apodaca, Don Sebastian, 52
Rum, 47, 56

ST. ANDREW, 63
ST. CROIX, 28–31
ST. DAVID, 63
ST. GEORGE, Trinidad-Tobago, 63
St. George's, Barbados, 42, 43
ST. JOHN, Virgin Islands, 28, 30–32, 41
St. John's, Antigua, 44
ST. KITTS, 8, 32, 37, 39, 41, 44
ST. LUCIA, 6, 9, 37, 39, 40, 41, 44, 45
ST. PATRICK, 63
ST. THOMAS, 28, 30, 31, 33
ST. VINCENT, 9, 37, 39, 41, 45, 49
Salt, 26
Sam Lord's Castle, 36
San Salvador, 7, 11, 12
Santo Domingo, 12
Scarborough, 53
Senate
  Bahamas, 14
  Barbados, 36
Slaves, 6, 9, 12, 28, 32, 36, 52
Solomon, Patrick, 53
Spain, 7, 8, 11, 27, 51
Sponges, 18
SPORTS, 61
Steel band, 59
Sugar, 47, 56, 62
"Tamboo Bamboo," 59
Terms of Capitulation, 52
"Thirsty Island," 43
Tortola, 31, 32
Tortugas, 23
Tourism, 18, 46, 64
Treaty of Aix-la-Chapelle, 9
Treaty of Amiens, 52
Treaty of Tordesillas, 8
Treaty of Versailles, 44
TRINIDAD AND TOBAGO, 5, 6, 9, 37, 38, 51–64
TURKS AND CAICOS ISLANDS, 6, 26
Turk's heads, 26
United Nations, 54
United States, 11, 12, 26, 28, 30
UNITED STATES VIRGIN ISLANDS, 28–31
University of the West Indies, 61
Valley of Desolation, 42
Venezuela, 6
VICTORIA, 62
Virgin Gorda, 32
VIRGIN ISLANDS, 5–7, 28–33
West Indies, 5
West Indies Federation, 37, 38
Williams, Eric, 53, 54
Windward Islands, 35, 37, 38, 40, 45

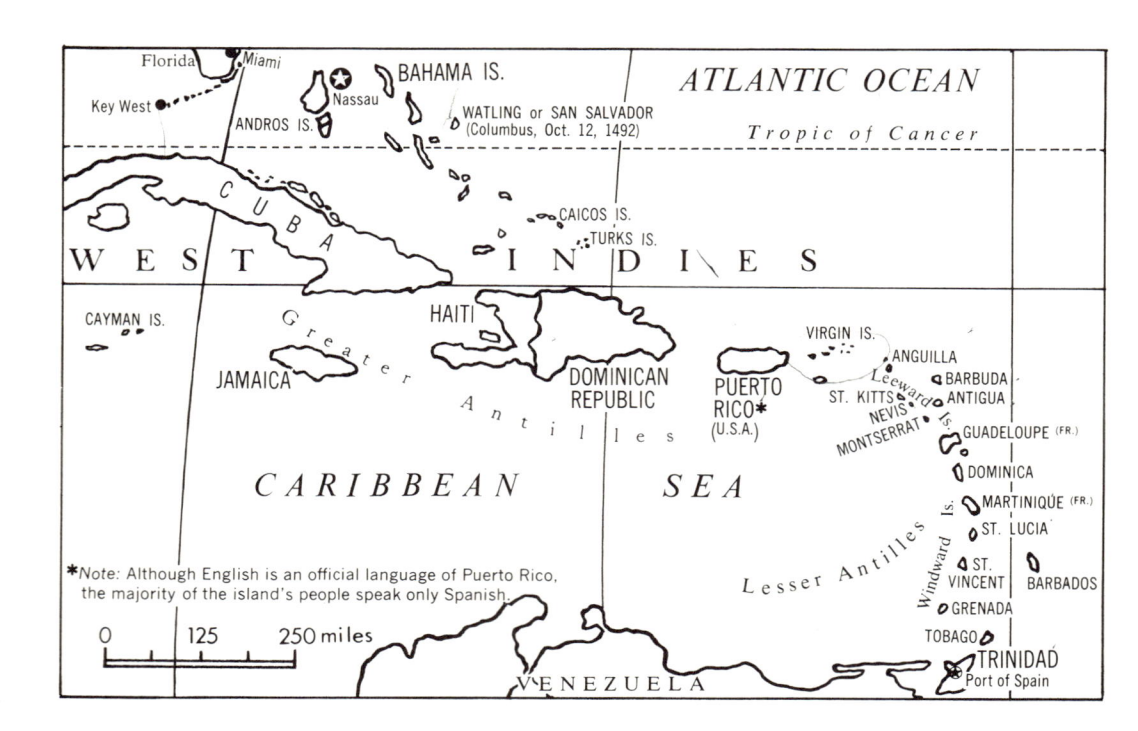

The picturesque port of Spanish Wells, now the home of peaceful fishing smacks, was once a port of call for the mighty galleons of Old Spain. The town is also one of the most attractive resorts in the Bahamas' Out Islands.

From the western tip of Tortola, the panorama of the Virgin Islands reveals the nature of the islands' formation—a submerged mountain chain.

INTRODUCTION

THE ISLANDS OF THE CARIBBEAN, collectively called the West Indies or the Antilles, are extremely varied in population, language, and cultural heritage. The scope of this book is limited to the English-speaking islands other than Jamaica, an island so large and populous as to constitute a study by itself. The remaining islands of Anglo-Saxon speech range in size from islets with only a handful of inhabitants, to Trinidad which has over 1,000,000 people living on almost 2,000 square miles of land.

Scattered over a vast area in and around the Caribbean, these islands have many distinct differences, and certain unifying factors. Most of them (the Bahamas are a notable exception) are exposed summits of a submerged mountain chain that is, in effect, a continuation of certain ranges of Central America. The Bahamas are low-lying and largely of coral formation, and are the northernmost of all West Indian islands, lying actually in the Atlantic rather than in the Caribbean. South and east of the Bahamas are the Virgin Islands, actually the beginning of the part of the chain called the Lesser Antilles. The Greater Antilles, comprising the four large islands of Jamaica, Cuba, Hispaniola, and

5

Puerto Rico, all lie together at the northwestern end of the undersea mountain chain. In an arc southward from the Virgin Islands, the islands of the Lesser Antilles sweep toward Trinidad and the coast of Venezuela. In this section many English-speaking islands alternate with those of Dutch or French speech. Thus the islands with which we are concerned here fall into four groups: the Bahamas and other islands at the northern end of the arc; the Virgin Islands; Barbados and other English-speaking islands of the eastern Caribbean; and Trinidad and Tobago. All of these islands share the English language (each with its own distinctive inflection); a predominance of African blood; a delightful climate where the tropical sun is constantly tempered by the cooling effect of the northeasterly trade winds; and a history in which slavery, plantation economics, buccaneering, and European power struggles are important factors.

The political structure of these islands is as complex as the cultural. Some are sovereign nations, as the Bahamas, Barbados and Trinidad-Tobago; others are associated states of the Commonwealth, still not fully independent, as Antigua, Dominica, Grenada and St. Lucia; half the Virgin Islands form a British Colony, the other half a Territory of the United States; Turks and Caicos and the Caymans have remained British Colonies. Attempts at forming federations among them have so far failed, owing to the far-flung geographical distribution of the islands and their differing economic needs. The differences are considerable, as will be seen subsequently.

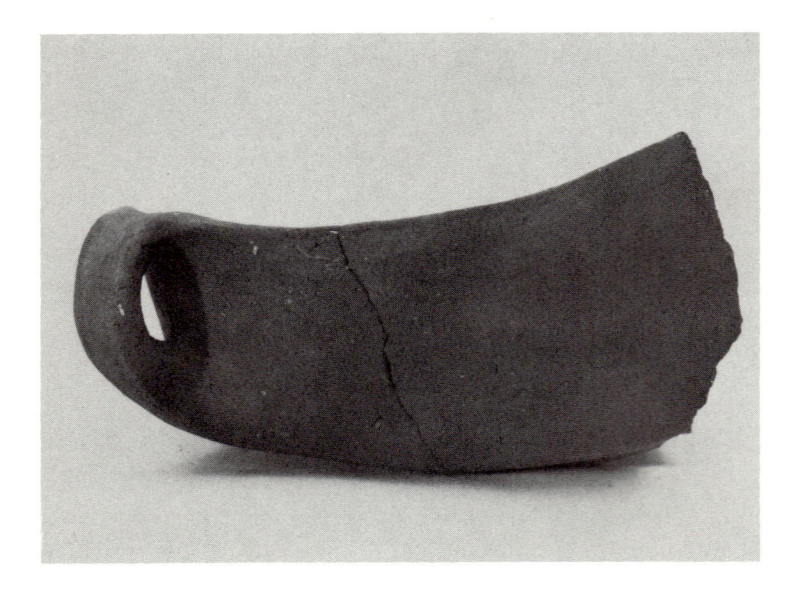

This potsherd, or pottery fragment, is of Arawak workmanship, a shattered reminder of a vanished race, unable to resist the onslaught of either the Caribs or Europeans.

A few miles from Cockburn Town, the principal settlement on the island of San Salvador in the Bahamas, this memorial marks the spot where, in 1492, Christopher Columbus first set foot in the New World.

HISTORY

In the summer of 1492, Columbus and about 100 men sailed from Spain in three small ships in search of a new trade route to the rich lands of eastern Asia. As a result of his lack of adequate geographical knowledge he found himself 36 days later on one of the islands of the Bahamas which he thought then was part of the East Indies. Later he sailed south and reached Cuba. He then turned east and sailed along the north coast of Hispaniola where his biggest ship was wrecked on a reef. He reportedly was forced as a result to leave a number of his men behind in a small fort built on the shore.

The following year, Columbus sailed again from Spain and his fleet of 17 ships reached Dominica and continued on from the Leeward and Virgin Islands to Puerto Rico. In 1494 during another short cruise he explored most of Cuba's southern coast and in that same year discovered Jamaica.

Three thousand miles away across open sea from Barbados' eastern coast lies the African continent, ancestral home of most Barbadians.

Under the Treaty of Tordesillas which was later signed by Spain and Portugal, Spain won the right to explore all the discovered lands west of the Cape Verde Islands. This line of demarcation explains why Brazil was colonized by Portugal and why Barbados, though discovered by the Portuguese navigator Pedro Campos in 1536, was never claimed or settled by Portugal.

The discovery of the New World lands by Columbus soon resulted in rivalry for their possession by other European nations. England occupied Bermuda in 1612, St. Kitts in 1624 and Barbados in 1625. Occupation by the English soon was the fate of Nevis, Antigua, Montserrat, Anguilla, Barbuda and part of the Bahamas. The French landed on St. Kitts shortly after the English, and for a while the two nations shared the small island.

Scholars have yet to unearth any recorded history of the West Indian islands prior to the discovery by Columbus. The first people in the West Indies of whom anything definite is known were the Arawaks and the Caribs. The tribes of Arawaks found in the various islands by the Spaniards were peaceful, unlike the more warlike Caribs. The Arawaks allowed the Spaniards to occupy their island homes without offering any significant resistance. The Caribs on the other hand fought fiercely against the Spaniards, French and English. In about fifty years after the arrival of the Spanish, the Arawaks became extinct because of their inability to survive under the harsh treatment meted out to them by the Spaniards who had enslaved them and because of battles with the Caribs.

In the meantime, the Caribs, particularly those on the island of Dominica, fought bravely and well against the Spaniards and others, and even used the island as a base from which to raid British and French colonies in nearby islands. After a bloody struggle in St. Vincent, a number of them were deported to Central America by the British. Later under the Treaty of Aix-la-Chapelle in 1748, it was agreed between Britain and France that because of the Caribs' savage hostility Dominica, St. Lucia, St. Vincent and Tobago should not be occupied by either nation but left to the Caribs.

In the wars that ensued despite signing of the Treaty, the islands involved were occupied by the contesting European Powers until final conquest by the British. By then nearly all the Caribs had been killed in battle or deported.

Today a few hundred Caribs survive in Dominica in a special reserve but many are of mixed blood. Others can be found in Guyana, British Honduras and other parts of Central America. As one historian states—"There is little to remind one in the West Indian Islands today of the Carib race which for three centuries resisted European pressure. The Caribs conquered and destroyed the Arawak race in the smaller islands, and were themselves conquered and destroyed by stronger people. . . ."

A legacy left behind by both the Caribs and Arawaks is a number of words which have come into common English usage. These include barbecue, buccaneer, canoe, cannibal, hammock, hurricane, iguana, potato and tobacco.

The story of the West Indies is also a saga of peoples being transported from their ancestral homelands to shape a new and uncertain future in a tropic clime. From the coastal areas of West Africa they were brought forcibly as slaves; from China and India they arrived as indentured workers. Europeans came as prisoners, exiles, fortune hunters, civil servants, traders, priests and farmers. The main period of European migration into the West Indies covered about 150 years. All these varied nationalities introduced into the islands their different languages, beliefs and systems of government.

The Spaniard brought his creed and system of government and his skill in the artful working of silver and gold. The English introduced the

A carved lion on a hillside is a reminder of the era when English troops were present in Barbados.

Elizabethan system of parliamentary procedures. The African brought his folk tales, beliefs, proverbs and music; the Frenchman, his system of law to St. Lucia and Dominica; and the Hindu, his temples and Muslim mosques to Trinidad.

Into the islands which form the Greater and Lesser Antilles were brought the African slaves, the group which followed the European migration. It is estimated that during the more than four centuries of forced migration an estimated 20,000,000 Africans were brought to the New World, many of these to the Caribbean islands.

The chiefly African heritage of the islands asserted itself in the late 1960's and early 1970's, when "black power" became an active political force. In Trinidad, Antigua, Grenada, Barbados and other islands, black people demonstrated against continued white control of industry, banking and trade.

BAHAMA ISLANDS

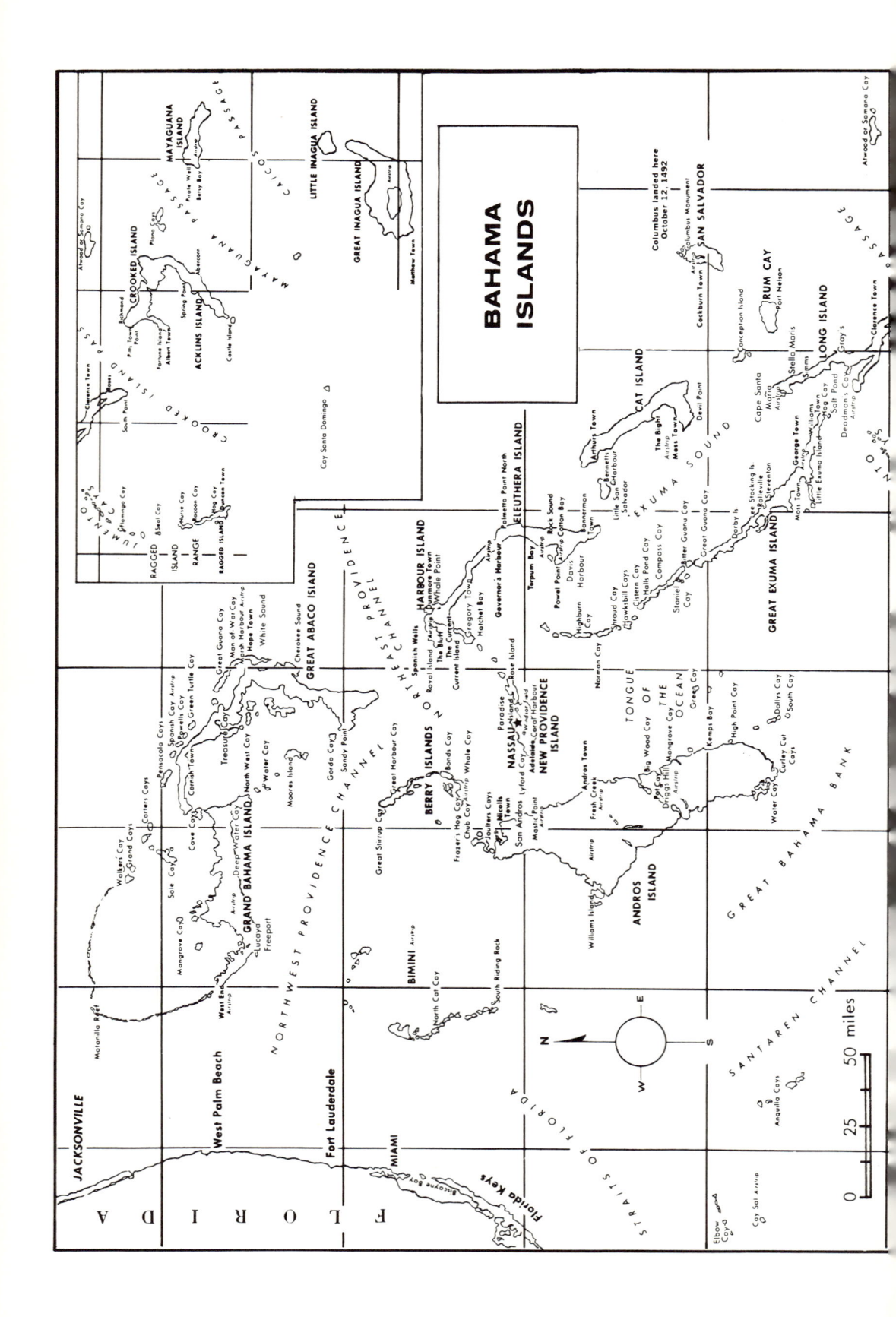

This church is on Eleuthera Island, where the English first settled in the Bahamas.

THE BAHAMAS AND OTHER NORTHERN ISLANDS

ON FRIDAY, OCTOBER 12, 1492, the explorer Christopher Columbus sighted the island in the Bahamas now known as San Salvador. It was the first of the New World lands he was to discover in the name of the throne of Spain. The Spanish made no attempt to colonize or settle in the Bahamas, but they transported the race of Carib Indians they found there to work in the mines of nearby Haiti and Cuba.

In 1629, England's ruling monarch, Charles I, gave the island to one Sir Robert Heath, but when the English attempted to settle there, they encountered opposition from the Spaniards. Twenty years later, a group of Englishmen called the Eleutherian Adventurers sailed into the Bahamas' Eleuthera Island and established a settlement there. Charles II in 1670 regranted the Bahamas to six lord proprietors who passed a law to punish pirates and as a result, in 1717, Captain Woodes Rogers of the Royal Navy, himself a former pirate, ordered all pirates on the island to surrender. It is said that some one thousand of the free-booters heeded the Captain's order. He pardoned many, and the others were hanged. Nassau for a very short while fell into American hands, when Commodore Hop-

The liveliest festival in the Bahamas is the Junkanoo, held on December 26 and January 2, which features marchers in fanciful costumes depicting various themes. These paraders represent atomic fission, "the ship of the desert," and the United States War of Independence.

kins of the American Navy captured the island but after holding it for a few weeks returned it unharmed to the English.

The Bahamas became prosperous when African slaves were introduced, but the planters experienced financial ruin when slavery was abolished in 1838. Nassau enjoyed another period of prosperity from 1861–65, the period of the Civil War in the United States, when it was used as a depot for guns and ammunition and other supplies for the Confederate States.

GEOGRAPHY

The Bahamas, an archipelago comprising some 700 islands and about 2,400 cays scattered over 70,000 square miles of sea, have a total land area of nearly 5,000 square miles, but only a dozen of the islands contain the bulk of the population. From the north of the island chain which lies approximately 60 miles off the Florida coast, the islands extend for some 500 miles in a southeasterly direction towards Santo Domingo. The names of the populated islands are well-known to the thousands of tourists who visit the Bahamas each year as they follow the sun. These include New Providence, Andros Island, the Abacos, Berry Islands, the Biminis, the Exumas, Rum Cay, San Salvador, Long Island, Mayaguana, Crooked Island, Grand Bahama, Eleuthera and the Inaguas, the most southerly of the Bahamas group.

Eleuthera Island was the home of the first English settlers. Scottish visitors say that the

Native sloops tie up at Nassau's Prince George Wharf where produce from the other islands will be sold at the bustling Waterfront Market.

island's hills and dales remind them of their homeland and, because of its extensive farming, it is also known as the bread-basket of the Bahamas. Nassau is located on the northern side of New Providence Island. It is the main commercial city and the seat of the Government. Grand Bahama, the fourth largest of the island chain, lies about 60 miles east of Palm Beach, Florida, and 145 miles northwest of Nassau. It has large areas of pine and other

13

Freeport on Grand Bahama, a booming year-round resort, offers a sheltered marina, luxury accommodations and many recreational facilities.

timber and is growing in importance commercially through the steady development of Freeport as an international holiday resort area. Freeport is located approximately 76 miles from Palm Beach and 120 miles from Miami. Even nearer to the North American mainland are the Biminis, a pair of small islands only 50 miles from Miami, noted as a haven for anglers, and, formerly, for pirates.

Andros Island, the largest of the Bahama group, is actually composed of several islands separated by narrow, shallow tidal channels and covered with large pine and mahogany forests.

CLIMATE

Located above and below the Tropic of Cancer, the climate of the Bahamas is not entirely tropical. However, the warm waters of the Gulf Stream keep the temperature consistently high to be comfortable during the winter period when the temperature averages 72 degrees F. and 85 degrees F. during the summer months.

GOVERNMENT

The Bahamas have had a form of representative government since the middle of the 17th century. An elected House of Assembly was established in 1729. Constitutional changes continued by degrees until January 7, 1964, when internal self-government was achieved. Under this new constitution, the Bahamas' governmental structure consists of a Senate and House of Assembly. There is a Governor representing the Queen, and a cabinet comprising the

An aerial view of New Plymouth Town on Green Turtle Cay, Abaco, shows the shallow lagoons, broad beaches and scrub forest typical of the Bahamas.

Government House in Nassau is the official residence of the Governor of the Bahamas. A statue of Christopher Columbus rises in the foreground.

The Nassau Police Band is an attractive spectacle for residents and visitors alike.

Premier and other Ministers, collectively responsible to the Legislature. The House of Assembly consists of 38 members. In 1967's general elections, the People's Political Party, headed by Lynden Pindling, defeated the formerly well-entrenched United Bahamian Party to give Bahamanians their first Negro government.

The new government undertook to amend the constitution further to obtain a greater measure of self-government, and changed the official name of the country to the Commonwealth of the Bahamas. To many observers, the islands seemed to be headed for full independence. Returned to office in 1972, Pindling announced plans for full independence and, in 1973, the Bahamas became a sovereign nation within the Commonwealth.

RELIGION

The Church of England (Anglican) is the State Church but many other denominations are strongly represented, including the Roman Catholic, Baptist, Seventh-Day Adventist and Presbyterian.

Yacht racing is a major tourist attraction in the Bahamas.

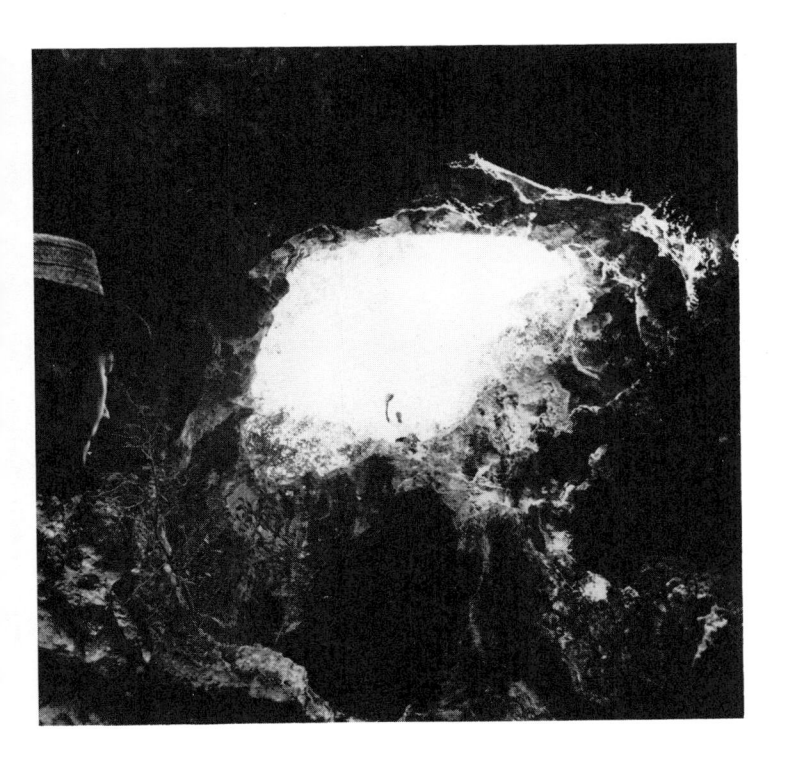

Preacher's Cave, on Eleuthera, once sheltered 17th-century castaways shipwrecked on the island.

Near Gregory Town, Eleuthera, a break in the reef sends turbulent Atlantic water into the placid lagoon known as the Glass Window.

Mosstown, in the Exuma group of the Bahamas, is situated in a fertile farming area.

POPULATION

The Bahamas population figure is approximately 168,000, the majority being of African descent. Distribution of the populace is somewhat uneven with over half of the total figure located in New Providence Island, and only 11 other islands inhabited by more than one thousand.

ECONOMY

The Bahamas' main source of revenue is tourism and its beautiful beaches and ultra-modern hotels attract thousands of American tourists each year. At one time the exportation of sponges was the islands' principal industry, but a blight made it necessary to close the sponge grounds in 1940. They have since been

Vehicles of all kinds proceed along Bay Street in Nassau.

A coconut grove provides a shady construction site for a sloop, at Mangrove Cay, Andros.

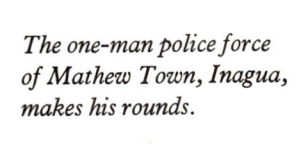

The one-man police force of Mathew Town, Inagua, makes his rounds.

The people of the tranquil, sunny island of Great Exuma grow sisal and from it weave straw baskets and purses for export. Great Exuma is also a rapidly developing resort area.

Joe Robins is regarded as the original of the hero of Ernest Hemingway's novel "The Old Man and the Sea." Here he stands before the house where Hemingway stayed on frequent visits to Bimini.

Unicycles, actually bicycles ridden on the rear wheel only, are popular with Bahamian youngsters. The onlookers seem to be afraid that this young resident of Nassau will lose his balance.

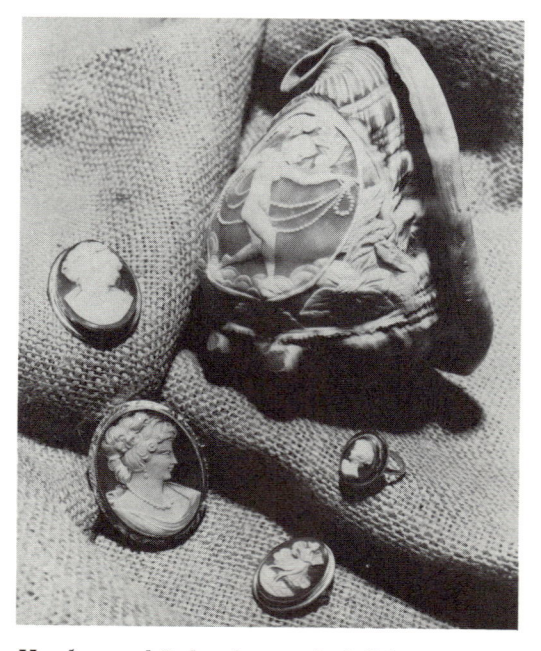

Hand-carved Bahamian conch shell is a speciality of the islands. The outer layer of the shell is white, while the inner layers are pink and coral—ideal for making cameos.

South Bimini's Inn and Marina are only a short distance from Miami, Florida.

re-opened, but the industry is much smaller than it used to be.

For a short period, agriculture played an important role in the islands' economy. This was after the American Revolution when some of the American colonists who had remained loyal to Britain during the war left the mainland with their slaves and settled in the Bahamas. There they established cotton plantations which flourished for a while, but due to soil exhaustion and insect pests, the industry became a failure.

Fishing is a major industry on Grand Bahama Island. Bananas are grown on a number of the islands, but most of the fruit comes from old Eleuthera Island. Citrus fruits, mostly for the local market, are grown in all the islands, and cucumbers are the major export crop from the Abacos and Andros.

A new industry began in 1970, when an oil refinery was completed at Freeport on Grand Bahama. The new plant can process 140,000 barrels of oil a day.

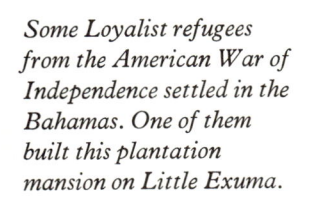

Some Loyalist refugees from the American War of Independence settled in the Bahamas. One of them built this plantation mansion on Little Exuma.

Fishing is not only a recreation, but also an important industry in the Bahamas.

The Bahamas Government uses its new decimal currency to advertise the country's natural charms and tourist attractions. The new money went into circulation in 1966, replacing the pounds, shillings and pence of the sterling currency in use since 1783.

At Rock Sound, Eleuthera, is an 1,800-acre ranch where cattle of the famous French Charolais breed are raised as breeding stock for U.S. cattlemen. These calves grow at the exceptional rate of four pounds a day.

In the village of Adelaide, near Nassau, children frolic in the schoolyard.

Craft items also are a big contributor to the Islands' economy. Sisal and coconut straw are used for weaving hats, mats, bags, and other souvenir items. Other such items in the form of jewelery and ornaments are made by native craftsmen from sea shells, fish scales and turtle shells.

CAYMAN ISLANDS

These three islands—Grand Cayman, Little Cayman and Cayman Brac—lie off the northwest tip of Jamaica, with which they formed a dependency until 1962, the year of Jamaican independence. The tie with Jamaica was severed at that time and the three low, coral islands remained a British Crown colony.

Like most of the other Caribbean islands, the Caymans were discovered by Columbus. However, Spain never colonized them and in time they were occupied by British settlers from Jamaica. Columbus called the islands the Tortugas (turtles) because of the large number of turtles found in the waters off them. Although the name of the islands has changed,

A drummer and a pianist-singer dispense songs of the Bahamas.

23

A quiet side street in Nassau typifies the serene temper of Bahamian life.

turtle fishing is still an important means of livelihood for the 9,000 inhabitants, along with the manufacture of thatch rope, and shark and sponge fishing. Bathing and fishing facilities are superb and tourism is being developed, but the main source of revenue comes from the money sent home by Cayman Island seamen, among the best in the Caribbean. A large part of the male population goes to sea.

Grand Cayman has an area of 76 square miles, Cayman Brac 14 square miles, and Little Cayman, 10 square miles. Cayman Brac has limestone bluffs reaching 140 feet in height, but the other islands do not exceed 60 feet in elevation. The thatch palm (source of the rope which accounts for half the colony's exports) and a native mahogany are typical trees of these sunny islands, whose temperature varies from 65 degrees to 85 degrees.

Georgetown on Grand Cayman, an attractive community of about 3,000 people, is the capital of the crown colony. Caymanians, as the Islanders are called, are mostly of mixed African and European race, although pure whites and blacks each constitute about 20 per cent of the population.

Nassau's tame flamingos perform for visitors in the Ardastra Gardens.

The guns of Fort Charlotte, 18th-century bastion in Nassau, are dramatically illuminated at night, in the course of a "Son et Lumiere" presentation, in which sound and lighting effects are used to highlight the history of the fort.

Apollo 9 astronauts landed on Eleuthera, where local children presented them with flowers and asked, "Can we go next time?"

Hovercraft, which ride above the water on jets of air, are a new means of fast transportation between the Bahamas' many islands.

TURKS AND CAICOS ISLANDS

These two groups of islands are geographically a southeastern continuation of the Bahamas. There are 8 islands in the Turks group and 22 in the Caicos, with a total area of 166 square miles.

All low-lying, many of the islands are uninhabited. Grand Turk Island (9 square miles) is the seat of government, and became famous in the 1960's as the re-entry point for orbiting United States astronauts after a United States Guided Missile Observer Station was established there. The islands are rather arid and not suited to agriculture other than growing sisal, salt-raking being the principal industry. Salt of very high quality is obtained by introducing sea water into shallow basins and letting the water evaporate under the strong tropical sun. A typical plant of the colony is a cactus whose flower resembles a red fez. Called Turk's heads, these plants gave their names to the Turks group.

The islands were originally settled by colon-

This giant "salina" or salt lagoon on Inagua Island in the Bahamas produces over half-a-million tons of salt a year.

The United States Guided Missile Observer Station on Grand Turk is the site of the historic re-entries from orbit of John Glenn and other astronauts.

ists from Bermuda, who started the salt-raking industry in 1678. The Spaniards had arrived first, Ponce de Leon having discovered the islands in 1512, but did not establish a colony. Part of the Bahamas from 1799 to 1848, the two groups became a dependency of Jamaica in 1874. When Jamaica became an independent nation in 1962, the Turks and Caicos Islands remained a British Crown Colony. The population of more than 6,000 is almost wholly Negro.

This uncluttered beach at Governor's Harbour, Eleuthera, is bordered by the lacy branches of casuarina trees.

At the end of April the city of Charlotte Amalie observes a week-long Carnival, when the flags of the four nations that ruled the Virgin Islands before the United States are flown, while steel bands lead nightly "traumps" or street dances. Here, clowns cavort during the Grand Parade, climax of the Carnival.

THE VIRGIN ISLANDS

IN 1493, during his second voyage to the New World, Christopher Columbus discovered the Virgin Islands. The 50 islands which comprise the chain have at one time or another been under Spanish, British, French, Danish, and Dutch rule.

UNITED STATES VIRGIN ISLANDS

The Virgin Islands of the United States consist of forty islands and cays, the largest of the islands being St. Thomas, St. John and St. Croix. Their combined land area covers 132 square miles with a total population of 62,000. The islands came under United States control in 1917 when they were purchased by the United States Government from Denmark for $25,000,000. The King of Denmark had previously bought St. Croix from France in 1733. The island of St. Thomas was notorious as a slave market. All three islands were held by the British during the Napoleonic Wars, but later were restored to Denmark.

ST. THOMAS

Second largest of the United States Virgin Islands, St. Thomas has a land area of 28 square miles. Its capital, Charlotte Amalie, has a population of nearly 30,000.

ST. JOHN

The island of St. John is 20 square miles in area, and it is there that is being developed the 29th National Park of the United States. The island's population figure is less than 2,000 of which 200 live in the settlements of Cruz Bay and Coral Bay, located on the island's eastern and western ends, respectively.

"Judith's Fancy," an early Danish sugar cane mill, is one of the landmarks on St. Croix, U.S. Virgin Islands. These relics of a once-flourishing industry dot the islands of St. Croix, St. Thomas, and St. John. Some have been converted into private homes.

ST. CROIX

The largest of the group is St. Croix with an area of 84 square miles and lies 40 miles across the water from St. Thomas. The island has a population of some 16,256. It is noted for its rolling hills, old windmills, and "old world" atmosphere. Alexander Hamilton served as an apprentice accountant in St. Croix in 1772.

GEOGRAPHY

The islands of St. Thomas and St. John have a mountainous terrain, the highest elevations rising to about 1,500 and 1,300 feet. St. Croix

Many-hued sails glide past Charlotte Amalie, the capital of the U.S. Virgin Islands, and a major cruise destination of the Caribbean, the only city on the island of St. Thomas.

29

rises on the north and east to 1,000 feet before sloping off to a low-lying plain along its southern coast.

CLIMATE

The islands have a healthy climate and 10 months of the year the heat of the sun is tempered by the easterly trade winds. An average mean temperature of 79 degrees F. prevails throughout the year and rainfall is moderate. An interesting fact about the islands is that they are free from almost all the common tropical diseases, and the island of St. John was declared by the Rockefeller Foundation to be one of the few places in the world free from the common cold.

ECONOMY

Tourism is the islands' leading industry. There are also several large rum distilleries and St. John is the main source of supply of bay leaves for the manufacture of the world-famous St. Thomas bay rum. Sugar cane cultivation and the production of sugar contribute to the islands' economy, and employ a substantial portion of their working force. St. Thomas and St. John also produce a large number of cattle for dairy and beef purposes.

The Steeple Building at Christiansted, chief town of St. Croix, is a museum of local history, with a large collection of Carib and Arawak relics.

The aerial tramway on St. Thomas provides a scenic ascent to 1,000-foot Flag Hill, with two pauses on the way up to permit a panoramic view of the bay, the capital city of Charlotte Amalie, and adjacent islands.

Trading schooners make the port of Christiansted, St. Croix, even more picturesque when combined with the delightful Danish architecture built on this, the largest of the three major U.S. Virgin Islands.

GOVERNMENT

The Governor of the Virgin Islands is appointed by the President of the United States. Under a new Organic Act signed by President Eisenhower on July 22, 1954, the islands are governed by a unicameral legislature of 11 members, designated Senators. Of these, two represent St. Croix; two, St. Thomas, and one, St. John, while the remaining six are "at large." Elections to the legislature are held every two years and the right to vote is given to the islands' residents who are citizens of the United States and are 21 years of age or over. Persons born in the Virgin Islands are U.S. citizens.

BRITISH VIRGIN ISLANDS

The territories which comprise the British Virgin Islands are Tortola, the largest, with a population of 7,500 and an area of 21 square miles. The other principal islands are Virgin Gorda, 9 square miles; Anegada, 13 square miles; Jost Van Dyke, 4 square miles; Salt Island, Peter Island, Guana Island, Bay Island, Little Thatch and Marina Cay. The island

Caneel Bay Plantation, a modern resort built around the structures of an old plantation, is the only facility of its kind on the otherwise uncommercialized island of St. John.

31

Camping and recreational facilities, such as this tranquil beach, abound on St. John.

group numbers 36, of which only 13 are inhabited.

Flanking the island of Tortola are many smaller ones including Deadman's Chest, historically associated with pirate lore of the Caribbean. Another of these islands, Norman Island, is claimed to be the Treasure Island of Robert Louis Stevenson's story.

CLIMATE

The British Virgin Islands are noted for their healthy climatic conditions. The average annual rainfall at Road Town, the capital of Tortola Island, is 49 inches. Average temperature in winter is 71 degrees F.–82 degrees F. and in summer 78 degrees F.–88 degrees F.

HISTORY

The Islands were discovered by Christopher Columbus in 1493 and he named them Las Virgines, in homage to St. Ursula, a Cornish lady who is said to have journeyed to Germany with 11,000 virgin attendants, and was martyred there with her entire retinue.

The history of the territories is closely linked with the exploits of pirates in the early years of European settlement in the West Indies. A Dutch group held Tortola until 1666, when a band of English adventurers captured it. In 1762, the Governor of the Leeward Islands annexed the island and forced its residents to move to nearby St. Kitts. In 1680 other planters with their families left the island of Anguilla and settled in Virgin Gorda. This movement was followed by other white settlers and in 1717 Virgin Gorda had a white population of over 300 and Tortola 159.

In 1773 the white planters were granted a civil government by England. The constitution provided a completely elected House of Assembly of 12 members, and a partly elected and nominated Legislative Council which met for the first time in 1774.

The Virgin Islands remained a part of the Colony of the Leeward Islands until July 1, 1956, when it was de-federated from the islands of Antigua, St. Kitts, Montserrat. The islands, however, still remained under the administration of the Governor of the Leeward territories.

POPULATION

Today the 9,000 people of the British Virgin Islands are principally of African origin, descendants of slaves. Europeans or Americans are fewer than 400 in number. Approximately 84 per cent of the population live in Tortola, 8 per cent in Virgin Gorda, and nearly 4 per cent each in the islands of Anegada and Jost Van Dyke. The other principal islands all have under 100 people.

GOVERNMENT

Under the present constitution the Islands are governed collectively through an Administrator, advised by an Executive Council, which consists of two official members, two elected members and one nominated. There is also a Legislative Council of two official members, six elected, and two nominated, with the Administrator as President of the Legislature.

ECONOMY

During the days of slavery the British Virgin Islands prospered with their thriving sugar and cotton industries. Since that period, however, the large estates have been broken up and the agricultural sector now consists of small-scale cultivation. The principal industry is stock raising for the export market. Crops currently produced include sugar cane, used locally for rum production, and limes, bananas and coconuts for the United States Virgin Islands market. Plans to expand the islands' tourist trade are well advanced. The islands' second largest industry for export is fishing. Manufacturing is on a small scale and includes seven rum distilleries, all of which are on the island of Tortola. Straw and basket work is also a growing industry and benefits a great many of the islanders financially.

Magens Bay, St. Thomas, U.S. Virgin Islands, is regarded as one of the finest beaches in the world. Its white sands, unusual shape, and striking view from surrounding hillsides make it one of the most frequently photographed of all the many beaches in this Caribbean area.

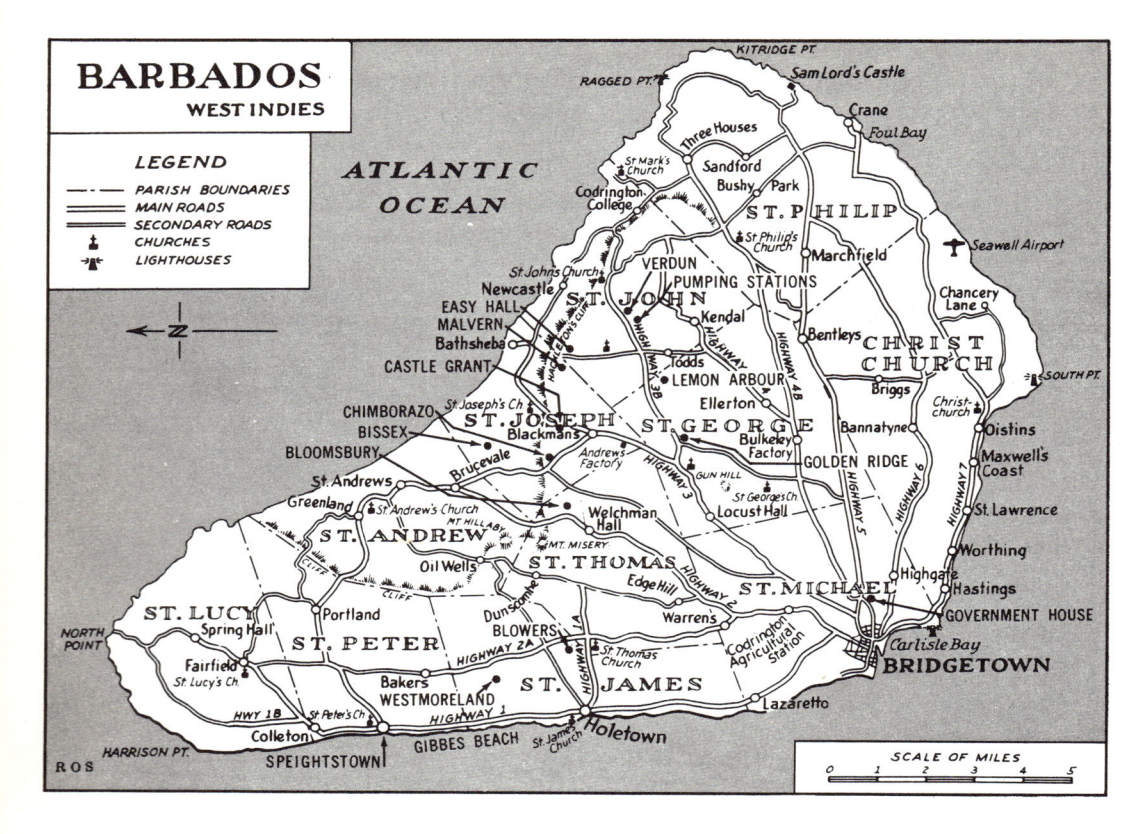

The quiet island of Montserrat is 10 minutes by plane from Antigua. Here the village of Bramble lies in the warm Caribbean sun.

The docks of Bridgetown, Barbados, are among the busiest in the West Indies.

BARBADOS AND THE ENGLISH-SPEAKING ISLANDS OF THE EASTERN CARIBBEAN

HISTORY

The islands of the Eastern Caribbean are called the Lesser Antilles and their history like the rest of the New World begins with the explorations of Christopher Columbus. Those to the south and east were historically called the Windward Islands, those to the north and west, the Leeward Islands.

Barbados, like Trinidad, an independent English-speaking island, got its name from the Portuguese mariner Pedro Campos. He landed on the island in 1536 and after noticing the abundance of fig trees there with long hanging roots, decided to name the island "Los Barbados" meaning "bearded." After leaving the island, however, Campos never returned. Later on, in 1625, Sir William Courteen's ship under the command of Captain John Powell arrived and claimed the island in the name of King James I of England. From this time on Barbados remained under British rule until independence was achieved on November 30, 1966.

The first 80 settlers landed at Holetown in St. James Parish in 1627. The location was known as Plantation Fort, and a stone monu-

Sam Lord's Castle in Barbados, now a luxury hotel, was once owned by the pirate Samuel Hall Lord, who built it in 1820.

ment still is there to commemorate the settlers' landing—a kind of Plymouth Rock in the tropics. Barbados grew into a thriving colony of 2,000 settlers by 1628 with a mixed population of Europeans and Negro slaves. The settlers first traded in tobacco and cotton and in 1640 came the introduction of sugar cane. Barbados' planters were the first in the Caribbean to establish large sugar plantations. One of the leading pioneer planters was James Drax whose name survives today in the district of Draxhall.

GOVERNMENT

Barbados as an independent member of the British Commonwealth functions through a Governor General representing the Crown, and a Prime Minister, the leader of the political party holding majority seats in the House of Assembly. On the advice of the Prime Minister, the Governor General appoints members of the Legislature as Ministers of Government. Barbados had its first Parliament in 1639 and without interruption has enjoyed a representative Government ever since. There is an Upper House or Senate comprising 21 members nominated by the Governor General on advice of the Major political parties for 5-year periods. The Lower House or House of Assembly has 24 members elected for 5 years. Two members are from each of the 11 parishes and two members represent the city of Bridgetown. The Prime Minister and his Ministers form the Cabinet.

The constitutional changes which eventually led to full independence in Barbados began between the two World Wars. One of the loudest voices for change belonged to the Democratic

League founded in 1923–24 by Dr. Charles O'Neale, some of whose followers were inspired by the ideas of Marcus Garvey, leader of the Back-to-Africa Movement. In 1938 another political party, the Progressive League was formed to add to the growing demand for wider constitutional reforms. The League later changed its name to the Barbados Labour Party with Grantley Adams, a barrister-at-law, as President. He was later to be knighted and became the first and only Prime Minister of the now defunct West Indies Federation.

Other political groupings later came on the scene, including the West Indian National Congress Party and the Conservative Elector's Association. Sir Grantley Adams, as leader of the dominant Barbados Labour Party which had won the 1951 general elections, became Barbados' first Premier when he again led the Barbados Labour Party to further victory in February 1954. Seven years later, the relatively new Democratic Labour Party led by barrister-at-law and ex-R.A.F. Officer Errol W. Barrow defeated the Barbados Labour Party and took over the Government under Barrow as Premier and Minister of Finance. Premier Barrow and his party went on to win the island's pre-independence general elections, and when independence was achieved on November 30, 1966, he became Prime Minister and Minister of Finance.

In 1967, following the example of Trinidad, Barbados became the second Commonwealth nation to join the Organization of American States.

FEDERATION

The political destiny of Barbados, Antigua, St. Kitts, Nevis, Anguilla, Dominica, St. Lucia, St. Vincent and Grenada appeared to have become interwoven for better or for worse in

Antigua's historical English Harbour served as a strategic base for ships of the Royal Navy assigned to the Windward Island area during the early 18th century.

Barbados Mounted Police are seen in formation outside the Legislative Building in Bridgetown.

April 1958 when they officially became units of the inaugurated West Indies Federation. The Federation was born out of high hopes by leaders of the area and included Trinidad-Tobago and Jamaica. By 1962, however, Jamaica and Trinidad-Tobago decided to seek independence on their own, and as a result of the loss of these two larger units, the Federation floundered and died.

It should be pointed out, however, that the federal concept of Government in the West Indies was not new. As far back as 1682 the area experienced a limited type of federation when the Leeward Islands actually formed a Federal Assembly. In 1876 attempts were also made to federate Barbados and the Windward and Leeward Islands but the plan proved unsuccessful when Barbados rejected the idea.

INDEPENDENCE

Since the Federation of the West Indies was dissolved in 1962, there was hope that from its

Policing the waterfront is the responsibility of Barbados Harbour Police. Barbadians are a very orderly people, with a markedly British sense of decorum.

Roseau is the chief town of Dominica. The island was named by Columbus, in 1493, who discovered it on a Sunday (Dies Dominica, the Lord's Day, in Latin).

For nearly a century England and France fought bitterly for possession of picturesque St. Lucia.

disintegration would come a Federation between Barbados, Antigua, Montserrat, St. Kitts, Nevis, Anguilla, Dominica, St. Lucia, St. Vincent and Grenada. However, Grenada withdrew from the talks on the possibility and Antigua did likewise in 1965. A few months later Barbados proposed to its Legislature that it should proceed to separate independence before considering the question of Federation.

After the achievement of independence by Barbados most of the other territories agreed on a new system of Government which they now enjoy. Under the new constitutional arrangements with the British Government each territory has achieved statehood in association with Britain, with control of its internal affairs and the right to amend its own constitution, including the power to end the association with Britain and declare itself independent.

So long as the territories remain states in association with Britain, the British Govern-

Ruins of Nelson's Dockyard in Antigua are a reminder of the era when the British Navy maintained the Throne's control of the sugar-rich Caribbean territories.

ment accepts responsibility for their external affairs and defence. Apart from these powers and responsibilities, and powers concerned with the application in the territories of the British Nationality Acts, the British Parliament has no power to legislate for the territories without their consent, and the British Government has no responsibility for the conduct of their internal affairs.

Montserrat remained a colony, however.

GEOGRAPHY AND POPULATION

Barbados, with a population of 300,000, covers a land area of only 166 square miles, as compared to Dominica's 289 square miles which makes the latter island the largest of the Windward–Leeward chain. Barbados which is the most easterly of all the islands lies not in the Caribbean Sea, but is located in the Atlantic Ocean, apart from the chain, with St. Lucia as its nearest link.

The land area and population figures of the other islands are as follows:—Antigua with its

Bridgetown Harbour Police, Barbados, still wear uniforms in the style of seamen of the late 18th century.

Rugged cliffs rise beyond the palm trees at Cars Bay on Montserrat. With abundant rain and rich volcanic soil, Montserrat is well-suited to raising cotton.

two dependencies, Barbuda and Redonda, 170½ square miles (Redonda contributing the half-square mile), population, 62,000; Dominica, 289.5 square miles, population 72,000; Grenada, 120 square miles, population, 103,000; Montserrat, 39 square miles, population, 15,000; St. Kitts-Nevis-Anguilla, 65, 36 and 34 square miles respectively, and a combined population of 60,000; St. Lucia, 238 square miles, population 108,000, and St. Vincent, 150 square miles, population 93,000.

Barbados, topographically, is the least volcanic of these islands and boasts a wide variety of scenic beauty. Its eastern coastline faces the Atlantic and its constant breezes resemble the Mediterranean climate rather than that of the tropics. The island's temperature normally ranges between 75 and 85 degrees F., rarely falling below 68 degrees or rising above 88 degrees. Temperatures are lowest in the period December to May and the months with the highest rainfall are January to June.

Clear skies and a placid sea help to make St. John's, Antigua's capital and commercial hub, a tropical delight for visitors.

The fishing boats come in at St. George's, Grenada, often described as the most picturesque town in the Caribbean.

Throughout the West Indies, an interesting climatic feature is the consistency of the high temperature from month to month. The coolest months are those when the sun is south of the equator, and even then the temperature rarely falls below 75 degrees from island to island. During hotter months, the average temperature is 80 degrees. The famous trade winds also help influence the area's temperature changes. Although the trade winds bring moisture across the land, they are not normally rain-bearing and so the typical Caribbean weather conditions are blue skies with cumulus clouds.

These islands where the trade winds play are noted for their natural beauty and the hospitality of their people. They are islands of mountains and hills, valleys and beaches, a combination which continues to attract vacationers from all over the world.

DOMINICA is ruggedly scenic with a high mountain range like a green backbone along its entire length, and with its highest point, Morne Diablotin, rising 4,747 feet above sea level. Dominica is undoubtedly the most mountainous of the islands which form the Lesser Antilles. It has been described as a land of peaks, ridges, and ravines and in proportion of mountainous terrain to total land area it is more rugged than Switzerland. Geologists have found hardly any non-volcanic rocks on the island, and the numerous hot streams there indicate that there is still some subdued volcanic activity. A boiling lake in the Valley of Desolation continues to spurt boiling water up to 10 feet and more. About three-quarters of Dominica is forested, the highest proportion of forest land in the West Indies.

Cane-field workers cut and load sugar cane, one of Antigua's main agricultural products.

ANTIGUA, described as the "Thirsty Island" because of its lack of rivers and lakes boasts a history linked with the exploits of the famous English Admiral Lord Nelson. In 1794, at the age of 26 years Nelson arrived there as Captain of a frigate, and on the seas around the island he drilled the crew in the manoeuvres which he was later to adapt against Napoleon's navy at the famous sea battle of Trafalgar. Since there are no streams of any significant size in the island, a great deal of work has to be done to provide water for local use through drilling of wells and

The port of St. George's is the capital of Grenada, "the isle of spice."

These fishing boats are part of St. Lucia's fast developing fishing industry.

by making ponds, reservoirs, and catchments in the hills. Not far from its capital, St. John's, are remnants of old volcanic mountains comprising a range of hills which rise to over 1,000 feet of which Boggy Peak is the highest (1,319 feet).

GRENADA with a thickly wooded terrain is wholly volcanic and its highest peak Mt. St. Catherine rises to nearly 3,000 feet. Its capital city is St. George's. **MONTSERRAT**, discovered by Columbus in 1493, was named by the explorer after a mountain in Spain on which is located the monastery where Ignatius Loyola planned the founding of the Roman Catholic Church's Society of Jesus. Like Grenada its topography is volcanic.

ST. KITTS, first of the British West Indian Islands to be settled acquired the title "Mother Colony of the West Indies." The Treaty of Versailles brought it under British rule. Its landscape is dominated by three volcanic peaks, one of which, Mount Misery, attains 4,314 feet. It is federated with Nevis and Anguilla.

NEVIS is an almost circular island with its central sector dominated by a volcano—Nevis Peak (3,232 feet). It is famous as the birthplace of Alexander Hamilton, first secretary of the United States Treasury and one of the founders of the Republic.

ANGUILLA, located about 60 miles north of St. Kitts is a low-lying coral island rising at its highest to a little over 200 feet. Anguilla attained brief renown in 1967 when it declared itself independent of St. Kitts, leaving its status uncertain. In 1969, the little island attracted world-wide attention when British troops invaded it to enforce membership in the Federation with St. Kitts and Nevis. To dissolve the Federation would require an Act of the British Parliament, a step which the British

Sugar cane harvesting in Barbados is a major occupation. Here a load of freshly cut canes is on the way to the mill.

Government is reluctant to take, and the question of Anguilla's status has remained unresolved.

ST. LUCIA, along with Grenada, St. Vincent and Dominica, is one of the four main islands in the Windward group. It is a volcanic island, extremely mountainous in the north and central areas. Hot sulphurous streams in the south show that volcanic activity there has not entirely died down. Two of the island's highest volcanic peaks, Grand Piton and Petit Piton which rise 2,619 feet and 2,461 feet above sea level respectively, are among the best known scenic features in the West Indies.

ST. VINCENT with its array of peaks, ridges, and ravines ranks next to Dominica as a mountainous island. The island is entirely volcanic in origin and it is there that can be found the peak of Soufrière, which reaches a height of 4,048 feet and is one of the two active volcanoes remaining in the Caribbean (the other is on French-owned Martinique). In 1902 its eruption killed 2,000 people, and devastated nearly a third of the island. Morne Garu, 3,523 feet, is also another volcano which dominates the island's terrain.

ECONOMY

Agriculture is still the main occupation of the peoples of the West Indies and will certainly be for a long time to come. This does not mean, however, that the governments of the various territories are not exploring and developing the

Deep Water Harbour, Bridgetown, Barbados, opened in 1961, greatly expanded the island's capacity to handle ocean traffic.

45

The waters around Barbados offer excellent year-round fishing for the sportsman.

potentials of other sectors to strengthen their collective economies.

The tourist sector is being steadily developed in the islands, and the building of hotels to meet the demands of that expanding industry is being pursued diligently with the help of overseas investors who see in Caribbean tourism a lucrative source of revenue.

The celebrated Barbados Fishing Tournament is in progress.

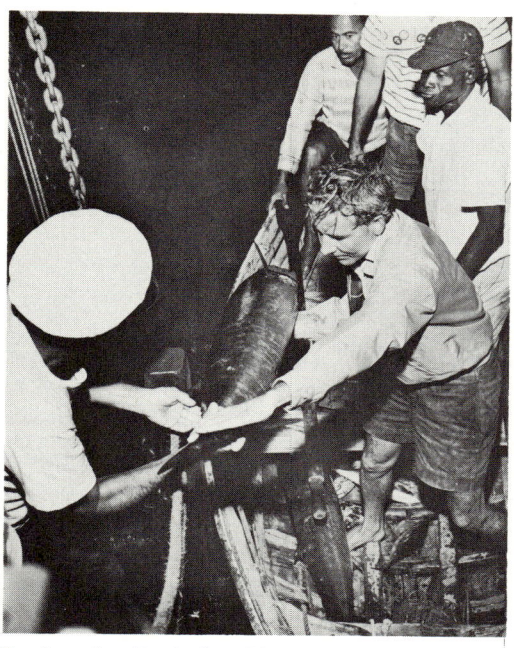

During the Barbados Fishing Tournament, an angler weighs in the catch at the Barbados Aquatic Club.

Mahogany plantations like this one are part of the scheme for development of forestry in Barbados.

Bananas and sugar head the list of agricultural crops providing the highest returns from the export market. In Barbados, the principal agricultural product is sugar, the fortunes of the island having depended on that commodity since 1660, when tobacco farming failed under competition with Virginia tobacco farmers. Barbados rum, a by-product of the sugar industry, is also world famous for its quality. Fishing is also an important activity, and the industry engages a fleet of 400 powered launches.

A recent survey shows that sugar cane grown

The Queen Elizabeth II Hospital, Barbados, symbolizes the island's drive toward better health and living standards.

Barbados' famed Codrington College, built more than a century ago, teaches medicine and theology.

Yachting is a popular sea sport in Barbados.

Young men engage in a game of cricket along the shoreline in Barbados.

48

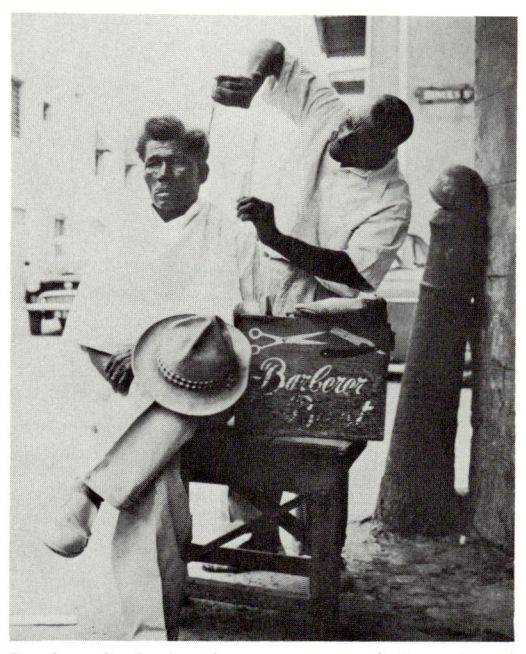

Outdoor barbering is one aspect of the relaxed way of life in Barbados.

Pottery is a highly developed craft in Barbados.

on 200 estates and thousands of peasant plots represent 85 per cent of the island's total visible exports. Sugar and bananas dominate the economy.

Montserrat's main crops include cotton, vegetables and citrus fruits, while on Anguilla the raising of sheep and goats is a means of making a livelihood from the land. In St. Vincent two-thirds of the populace depend on agriculture for employment and after bananas, the secondary products include nutmegs and cocoa.

In Antigua an estimated 12,000 acres are under sugar cane cultivation. In-shore fishing for the local market also plays an important role, as does the cultivating of sea-island cotton. Coconuts, cocoa, vanilla and limes contribute to Dominica's export trade, but bananas are the island's principal cash crop.

Water-skiing off West Coast Beach, Barbados, is one of the many recreational facilities that make the island a fine place to spend a holiday.

49

TRINIDAD

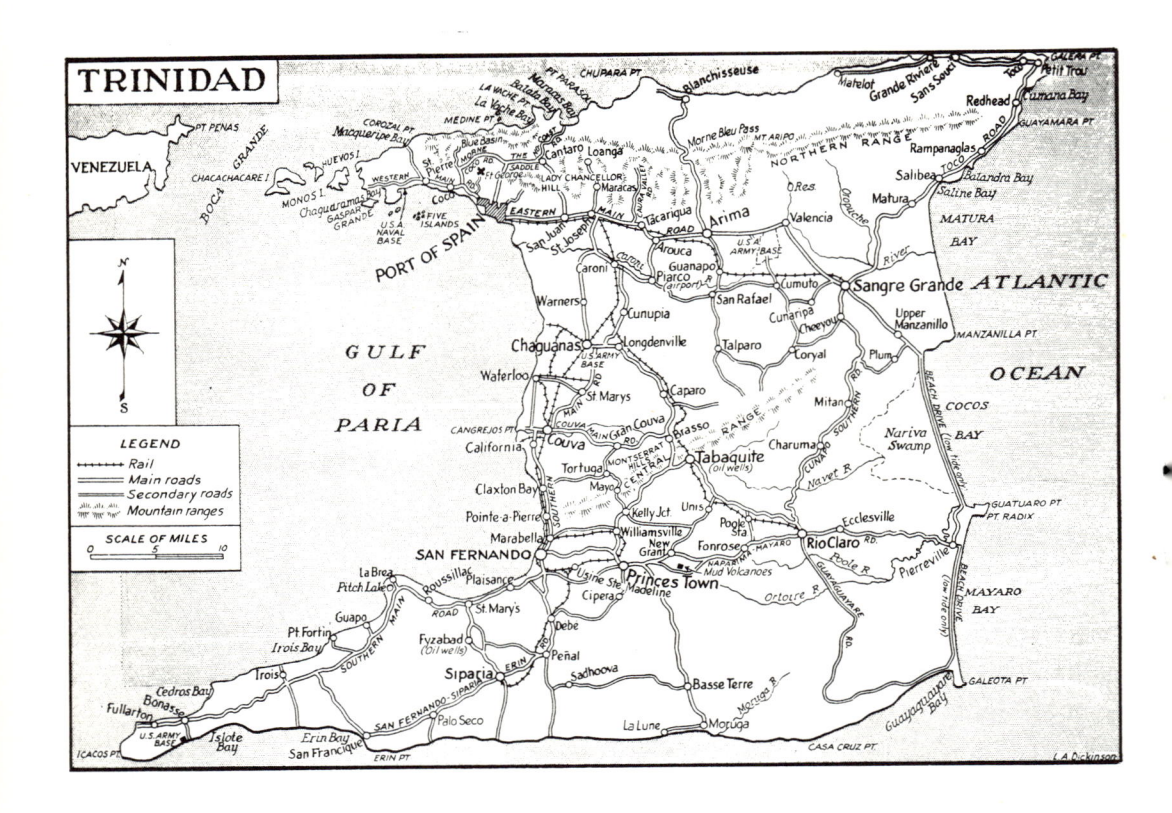

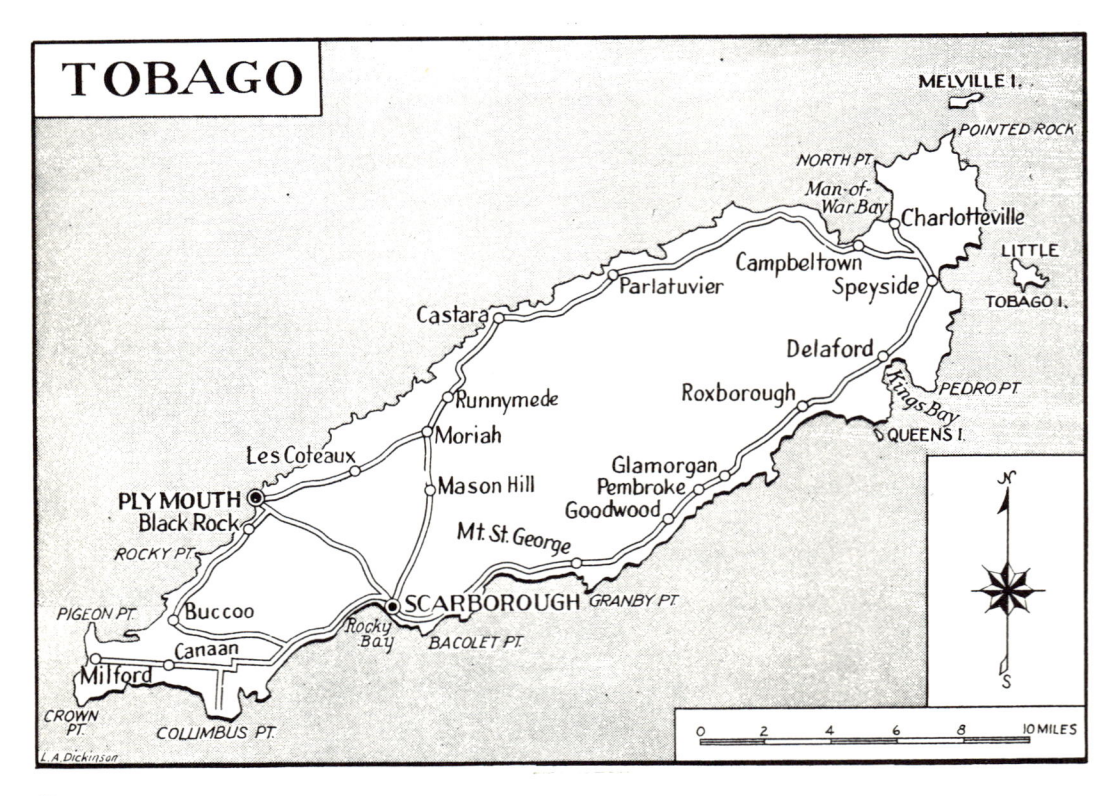

TOBAGO

Strollers find tree-shaded Hyde Park in Port of Spain a welcome escape from the midday heat.

TRINIDAD AND TOBAGO

IT IS SAID that when Christopher Columbus sighted the island of Trinidad on his third voyage to the New World he gave it that name in dedication to the "Holy Trinity" because of the three mountain peaks he first saw rising along its southern coast.

It was on July 31, 1498, four years after he had discovered Jamaica, that Columbus found Trinidad but did not land. The island at that time was inhabited by two groups of Indians, the Arawaks and Caribs. The latter called their Caribbean homeland "Iere" which means "the land of the hummingbird," an exotic term which is still used by many when referring to Trinidad. The peaceful Arawaks were later killed off by the warlike Caribs.

Thirty years had elapsed after Columbus discovered Trinidad before the first Spaniards attempted to colonize it. The first permanent settlers arrived in 1584 and established themselves on the banks of the Caroni River. This slow development was due mainly to the fact that the island had no mineral wealth to attract settlers. Those who had arrived and established plantations, nevertheless, faced many problems including frequent attacks by English, French and Dutch raiders. The planters' chief export crop, cocoa, which they found growing wild and had cultivated extensively, was struck by disease. Gradually many settlements were abandoned and by 1733 the number of Spaniards left on the island fell from several thousand to less than 400.

In 1770, in view of the island's potentials in agriculture, a petition was made to the King of Spain to open the island to immigrants. As a

51

result, in 1783, a Royal Cedula or permit for colonization was issued and an influx of foreigners arrived to take advantage of the opportunities offered. These included land grants with special concessions to those who also brought in slaves. The French Catholics in particular arrived in large numbers from various areas including Canada and the Lesser Antilles. Later there were refugees from the revolutions which had swept France and Haiti. The settlers brought to their new homeland coffee and new varieties of cocoa and sugar cane.

THE ENGLISH

In 1797, Spain having declared war on Britain, an expedition under Sir Ralph Abercrombie and Rear Admiral Harvey was ordered to capture Trinidad. The Spanish ships of war were anchored at Chaguaramas under Rear Admiral Don Sebastian Ruiz de Apodaca. The Spanish Admiral, seeing his fleet bottled up in the bay with no means of escape, decided to burn his ships in the bay rather than to engage the British fleet, which was much larger in numbers than his. Only one Spanish ship, the *San Damasco*, was captured before the damage was done.

On February 17, the British force landed and surrounded Port of Spain. The Spanish Governor Don Maria Chacon, with his small force, had to capitulate, and the Terms of Capitulation were signed at Valsyan, St. Joseph. Trinidad became a British colony when it was ceded to Great Britain by the Treaty of Amiens in 1802, ending 300 years of Spanish rule.

Although slavery in the Caribbean was on the decline when the British took possession of Trinidad, they brought in many slaves to develop the fruitful land, and soon many of the great British fortunes were in the making. Incidentally, one of the Negro groups imported by the British government in the early days was a group of escaped United States slaves who had helped the British in the War of 1812. Until the Cedula on Colonization there were only an estimated 302 slaves in Trinidad. After the influx of immigrants, however, the slave population on Trinidad and Tobago reached 26,517.

Following the passage of the Emancipation of Slaves Bill by the British Parliament in 1834, the Negro was induced to leave agriculture and the resulting shortage in the manpower supply brought about subsidization of the immigration of some 145,000 East Indians to Trinidad under the indenture system. This meant that the government paid for the passage of the immigrant on condition that he sign a contract agreeing to work in the colony for a specified time. Many remained in the island at the end of their indenture period when they were offered land in place of their passage home. An earlier attempt had also been made to bring in natives of China and Portugal as indentured workers, but proved less successful than the scheme for recruiting East Indians.

CROWN COLONY STATUS

For the first century under the British, the average Trinidadian had virtually no power in industry or politics. As late as 1936, sugar and oil field workers had no trade unions. A Workingmen's Association which was formed in the

Built in 1906, the "Red House," located on Woodford Square in Port of Spain, is the seat of government for Trinidad and Tobago.

The town of Scarborough is Tobago's capital and chief port.

1890's suffered rapid decline when its leaders were arrested by the police after a riot in 1903.

Trinidad continued to be a ward of the British Colonial Office long after other Caribbean colonies were able to secure some limited form of representative institutions. It had no elected members in its Legislative Council until 1924. At the time of the 1937 riots only 6 per cent of the people could vote under property qualifications for nine seats in the Council, while the English Governor and the Crown continued to select ten of the Council's members and all of the island's Executive Council. For ten years through World War II no election was permitted although its sister colony Jamaica had long since won universal suffrage for its lower house.

NEW CONSTITUTION

On March 21, 1946, Trinidad was granted a new Constitution which gave its people universal suffrage in voting for more representatives in a legislature of 14 members. In June of the same year, the first election under the new Constitution was held, but no single bloc or party won a majority. The existing political groupings at that time were the West Indian National Party, The East Indian National Council and the Federated Workers Trade Union. In 1950 Trinidadians went to the polls under a more advanced Constitution which gave the country a ministerial system of government, similar to that of Great Britain.

THE PEOPLE'S NATIONAL MOVEMENT

In January 1956 the political climate of Trinidad-Tobago was changed with the formation of a new political party, the People's National Movement (P.N.M.) with the world-famous cricketer Learie Constantine as Chairman, Dr. Eric Williams as Political Leader and, later on, Dr. Patrick Solomon as Deputy Political Leader. In the general elections which followed on September 24, 1956, the P.N.M. won 13 of the 24 seats and became the first party government in Trinidad-Tobago. The Party was again victor in the general elections held on December 4, 1961 by winning 20 out of the 30 seats contested.

In 1969, Learie Constantine was elevated to the peerage by Queen Elizabeth II, and took his place in the House of Lords as Baron Constantine—the first black peer in British history. He died in 1971.

Immediately following the 1956 elections, the People's National Movement successfully prevailed upon the British Colonial Office to abolish the Crown Colony system which had for such a long period throttled the political aspirations of the peoples of Trinidad and Tobago. As a result, the system of nomination to the local legislature was modified to include among the five nominated members two People's National Movement members selected by the leader of the Party, who was also the Chief Minister. In 1959 the Executive Council was renamed the Cabinet, presided over by the Chief Minister. The Governor then ceased to be a member of the Cabinet and the ex-officio members (those who were members by virtue of holding a certain office) were not allowed to vote.

Full internal self-government followed after the General Elections of December 1961. A bicameral (two-house) legislature was introduced, all Lower House being elected, and Upper House members being nominated. Led by the People's National Movement Party and Prime Minister Dr. Eric Williams, Trinidad and Tobago achieved complete independence on August 31, 1962 but remained within the Commonwealth.

GOVERNMENT

The Constitution of Trinidad and Tobago provides for the appointment by the English throne of a Governor-General, and for a bicameral legislature. The 24 Senators are appointed by the Governor-General on the advice of the Prime Minister and the Leader of the Opposition. The 36 members of the House of Representatives are elected by universal suffrage. The Governor-General appoints as Prime Minister that member of the House of Representatives who, in his opinion, is best able to command the support of the majority of the House.

EXTERNAL AFFAIRS

Trinidad and Tobago chose to remain within the British Commonwealth after independence. It is a member of the United Nations and became a member of the Organization of American States (OAS) in 1967, the first Commonwealth country to do so. Trinidad and Tobago had also joined the Federation of the West Indies when it was formed in January 1958, and remained a member until it was dissolved on May 31, 1962. The nation is also represented by High Commissioners in other Commonwealth countries (United Kingdom, Canada, Jamaica, and Guyana). Representation in Washington, D.C. and Ethiopia is by Ambassadors.

TOBAGO

With a population of 35,000, Tobago, unlike Trinidad, was never a Spanish colony, but nevertheless was one of the most fought-over of all West Indian islands and changed hands innumerable times between the Dutch, French and English. Finally coming under British rule by 1803, Tobago had its own Legislature and Governor for many years. It was not until its

The first Prime Minister of independent Trinidad and Tobago, Dr. Eric Williams (left foreground) is received by officials of the United Nations in New York. A leader of the People's National Movement, Dr. Williams has guided his country toward greater participation in inter-American, as well as Commonwealth, affairs.

Tobago's Charlotteville is one of the finest natural ports in the Caribbean.

single-crop economy (sugar) failed that it was linked politically to Trinidad in 1889.

Tobago lies 19 miles northeast of Trinidad, 120 miles from Barbados and 75 miles from Grenada. It is 26 miles long and $7\frac{1}{2}$ miles broad, with an area of 116 square miles (74,392 acres) of which about 42,000 acres are under cultivation. The formation of the island is volcanic. The chief towns are Scarborough (population 15,000), Plymouth and Roxburgh. About $1\frac{1}{2}$ miles to the northeast is Little Tobago or Bird of Paradise Island, the only place in the Western Hemisphere where these birds can be seen in their wild state.

CLIMATE

Trinidad lies about 10° to 11° north of the equator so its temperature range is less than that of the islands farther north. Temperature is lowest in January when it averages 77 degrees.

The rainy season generally begins towards the end of May and lasts until November. A dry period often occurs for about two weeks in September or October. March is the driest of the twelve months. Trinidad and Tobago are practically free of storms and volcanic activity and tidal waves are unknown.

ECONOMY

Sir Walter Raleigh may have been the first man in the oil business in Trinidad. On one of his forays into the area he is said to have discovered the now famous lake of natural asphalt near La Brea (Sp. tar), careened his ships nearby and used the tar for caulking. This lake, which covers some 95 acres, has been worked for many years; it now employs several hundred men, and earns a worthwhile share of the nation's foreign exchange.

Asphalt is only a small part of the oil industry, which includes crude oil, natural gas and refinery products, as well. In all, the industry provides 30 per cent of Government's revenue and 30 per cent of national output of total

Pitch Lake is one of Trinidad's most important natural resources. During the past 70 years it has supplied 15,000,000 tons of asphalt for streets from Lake Shore Drive in Chicago to the Champs Elysées in Paris.

domestic income and 80 per cent of Trinidad's trade. However, in recent years substantial increases in production have been made possible by exploitation of offshore deposits—particularly in the Solado field located in the southern part of the Gulf of Paria, discovered in 1955.

AGRICULTURE

Although petroleum provides the major source of income on Trinidad, it employs less than 15 per cent of the worker force. A much larger fraction of that force, some 20 per cent, works on the land. Agriculture is second only to oil in terms of its contribution to the over-all economy. Sugar is one of the oldest crops, and still one of the most important. Production of rum as a by-product of sugar has been close to 3,000,000 proof gallons annually. Because of increasing local consumption and the increased storing of rum for aging, exports in recent years have been only slightly over 400,000 gallons.

Until the 1930's, cocoa was Trinidad's chief agricultural export. A widespread cocoa disease in the 1920's cut crop output drastically and exports, which amounted to 33,000 tons in 1921, fell to 3,000 tons in 1946. But higher world cocoa prices after World War II encouraged more planting of disease-resistant types of cocoa and a Government cocoa plan has done much to rehabilitate the industry.

Despite the fact that Trinidad and Tobago produce and export food products, including citrus fruits, coffee, bananas and coconuts, as well as cocoa and sugar products, a large percentage of food consumed on the islands must be imported. For this reason, as well as to provide additional employment, the Government provides technical assistance and helps to finance capital investment in agriculture.

INDUSTRIAL DEVELOPMENT

The many Government aids to industry constitute a major factor in the island nation's industrial growth. Such development projects started with the Aid to Pioneer Industries Ordinance of 1950, which was the first of a series of laws designed to encourage investment in new industrial enterprises, and tourist trade.

On a coconut plantation a Trinidadian is hard at work removing the shells.

These laws provide for the duty free import of materials and equipment, income tax relief on profits for a minimum period of five years, allowance for depreciation of plant and machinery and for expenditure on research.

Another landmark in the Government's plan was the creation, in 1959, of the Industrial Development Corporation (I.D.C.) which acts as a liaison between investors and various Government departments. In addition, the corporation operates six industrial estates on which investors may lease sites. Generally the I.D.C. is reponsible for preparing the site and providing access roads, water, and electricity. Many of the more important new investments in Trinidad since 1959 were the result of the energetic promotion of the I.D.C.

THE PEOPLE

The people of Trinidad and Tobago are the product of many races, cultures and histories. The racial background of the area's 1,100,000 population is estimated at 43.5 per cent Negro, 36.4 East Indian, 16.2 mixed, 1.8 white, and all other groups 2.1.

A worker packs bottles of Trinidad's famous angostura bitters for export. The bitters, used in medicine and beverages, are extracted from the bark of a native tree.

Although much less important than other forms of agriculture, cattle raising nevertheless contributes to the Trinidadian economy.

Trinidadians have been described as being "British in character but Latin in disposition and cosmopolitan in appearance." The Spaniards have left behind names of places like San Fernando, Manzanilla and Sangre Grande, and a few villages in the rural areas still speak a kind of Spanish patois. The Spaniards also left a legacy in music and musical instruments. A French patois is also spoken in certain areas and the dominant Roman Catholic religion underscores the former French and Catholic influence. The festivals of the various racial and religious groups are all observed—Catholic, Hindu and Moslem mark their holy days.

ART, MUSIC AND CARNIVAL

Trinidad's Carnival is one of the outstanding festivals of its kind in the world. Taking place on the two days prior to Ash Wednesday, it has a long and interesting tradition over the past 200 years, beginning under Spanish rule. Then the influence of large numbers of French settlers tended to make it a national festival with the season running from Christmas to Ash Wednesday. In those days and up to 1833 the Carnival consisted mainly of elegant bands on foot or in carriages going from house to house visiting friends. Masked and fancy-dress balls were frequent.

Energy for Trinidad's growing industry comes from new thermal power stations such as this one at Port of Spain.

Steel band music is heard at its best in Trinidad, birthplace of this unique musical form.

Eastern bazaars add an exotic touch to Trinidad's shopping facilities. Here a lady in a sari examines typical East Indian brassware.

With the Emancipation of the slaves in 1834 Carnival became less exclusive. Festivities are said to have degenerated considerably during this period but in the 1890's took an upward turn developing into the great national festival that it is today with the participation of huge historical bands, artistic fancy sailor bands, and thousands of people masquerading as wild Indians, clowns, bats, and devils.

Within recent years a high degree of craftsmanship has developed not only in costume presentation but in metal, decorative leather and bead work, wire bending to provide the bases for papier mâché reproductions, embroidery and many other skills. But Carnival today means, at home and abroad, two unique art forms in which Trinidad has led and is teaching the world—the calypso and the steel band.

The steel band was evolved in Trinidad from a variety of ways to make music, dating back to the days of slavery, when drums were banned and so men resorted to "Tamboo Bamboo," or drums improvised from thick sections of bamboo. A tradition developed of making musical instruments from whatever material was at hand, and in time metal containers such as oil drums became the preferred source. Now the steel band is a national art form.

Tremendously interested in all human activity, and all branches of learning, the people of Trinidad and Tobago are organized into a great number of clubs, societies and associations that encourage, aid and foster activities as divergent as cycling and philosophy, music and natural history, chess and drama, art and football, writing and the dance. Cultural and religious observances often overlap and become interwoven with recreation in Trinidad. The Islamic ceremony of the Hosein festival attracts spectators of every creed, and often those who are neither Indian nor Moslem assist in the construction of the exquisitely intricate Taj, or Moslem shrine, in each community.

Interest in the visual arts, creative writing and the theatre has developed considerably. In the case of painting, this has now reached a point where the creative artist can find innumerable opportunities throughout each year to show his work. Enthusiasm for music and drama is wide-

Muslim mosques like this one, as well as Hindu temples, dot the island of Trinidad, whose population is more than one-third East Indian.

spread. The Trinidad Operatic Society produces light opera several times a year. The Christmas pantomime which contains a great deal of local custom has become an annual event; it is one of the many productions the Trinidad Dramatic Club puts on each year. The Music Festival and the Festival of Arts, presented in alternate years, have become regular features of the national life.

EDUCATION

The public primary and secondary schools and teachers' colleges of Trinidad and Tobago are of two types—denominational and governmental, although the costs of church schools are almost entirely borne by the Government. This dual control of the public education system is almost a century old. Almost all educational policy is prescribed by the Minister of Education and Culture, but each denomination has some say in the management of its schools. Education is governed by an Education Act.

Almost all children between the ages of 5 and 15 are in some form of school, whether private or public, primary or secondary. No fees are charged in government-operated or government-aided schools. In Port of Spain and San Fernando there are technical institutes which train persons in a wide range of skills: engineering trades, building trades, home economics, graphic arts, surveying, etc. A small training institute at Point Foitin prepares craftsmen for industry. In addition, very progressive training courses are carried on by firms such as the

The General Hospital in Port of Spain is an example of modern health facilities on the island.

electricity corporation and the oil companies. A school of agriculture and forestry trains middle-level technicians in these fields.

Trinidad and Tobago contribute to the University of the West Indies which has branches in Kingston, Jamaica and in Barbados as well as in Port of Spain. The Trinidad and Tobago branch specializes in engineering, agriculture and arts and science, and has recently set up an Institute of International Relations.

All students of Trinidad and Tobago enrolled at colleges have their fees paid by the Government. The four types of engineering degrees granted by the University are: chemical, mechanical, civil and electrical.

An adult education service is provided more for the upgrading of ambitious adults, than for the eradication of illiteracy. The training of teachers for primary and lower grades of secondary schools is done at five teachers' colleges. Other teachers are trained at the local university or universities abroad, particularly in the United Kingdom, the United States and Canada.

SPORTS

Although cricket is the national game, there are about 150 sports clubs and organizations in Trinidad and Tobago representing diversified interests. Among the most popular are football, field hockey, cycling, track events, tennis and swimming. In recent years field and track sports have become increasingly popular with both men and women and there are now many organized inter-club, inter-island and international meets.

Victorian architecture, such as the Queen's Royal College in Port of Spain, blends harmoniously in Trinidad with the modern, Spanish and Oriental.

GEOGRAPHICAL DIVISIONS

The total area of Trinidad and Tobago is 1,980 square miles, of which Trinidad alone accounts for 1,864. Trinidad itself is divided into eight counties: Caroni, Nariva, Mayaro, Victoria, St. Andrew, St. David, St. George and St. Patrick. These are subdivided into twenty-nine wards with Tobago as the thirtieth.

CARONI has an area of some 215 square miles and contains four wards. About 70 per cent of its population are of East Indian descent, while Spanish is still widely spoken in the Montserrat ward. Sugar-cane growing is the main occupation, but there are cocoa and citrus plantations, and coffee and coconuts.

NARIVA has an area of 64 square miles and is divided into two wards. There are large oil deposits and the forests yield valuable timbers. Agricultural production includes cocoa, rice and coconuts.

MAYARO has an area of 150 square miles with two wards. Oil was first drilled in the island in the Guayaguayare Ward where it is still produced. The Lagoon Bouff, a small pitch lake, is the main natural attraction.

VICTORIA has an area of some 314 square miles and five wards. It is the second most populous and prosperous part of the island, and its main town, San Fernando, is second to Port of Spain. The Pointe-à-Pierre ward contains the Texaco Oil refinery, the San Fernando Technical College and is also noted for its sugar production. Other crops include cocoa, rice and maize. Savana Grande ward also produces sugar cane and its forests are a source of valuable timber. Petroleum is found in large quantities in both

Maracas Beach is one of many popular bathing sites in Trinidad.

Fruits and vegetables are displayed and sold throughout Trinidad and Tobago at outdoor markets such as this one.

"Coconut water" (the juice of the unripe coconut) is a salable thirst quencher in Trinidad and other Caribbean Islands.

the Ortoire and Moruga wards. The main tourist attraction of the county is the Devil's Woodyard, a mud volcano or salse, not a true volcano, but a vent in the earth from which gas bubbles up through mud, causing the mud to form a cone.

ST. ANDREW has an area of 286 square miles and five wards. The main town, Sangre Grande, was important in the days when cocoa was the island's main agricultural product. Cocoa is still the main crop in the county, with coffee and coconuts and some petroleum deposits. The Guacharo Caves in Valencia ward are a popular tourist attraction.

ST. DAVID has an area of 78 square miles and a single ward. Its chief products are cocoa, coffee and coconuts and its forests yield cabinet woods.

ST. GEORGE together with the islands of the Gulf of Paria forms the northwestern district of the island, and has an area of 352 square miles. It comprises six wards and contains the capital, Port of Spain, with 100,000 people in 1970; the third town, Arima; the Five Islands and the Bocas Islands, mainly holiday resorts. There are a number of places of beauty and interest including the fine bathing beaches at Maracas Bay, Las Cuevas Bay and Blanchisseuse on the north coast. The northwestern and southern central area of the county are largely residential while the eastern districts are mainly agricultural, producing sugar cane, cocoa, coffee and coconuts; fishing is an important industry on the north coast. Piarco International Airport is in the ward of Tacarigua.

ST. PATRICK has an area of 260 square miles, and four wards. The major portion of the wealth of Trinidad and Tobago is produced here in the numerous oilfields. Fyzabad is the hub of the oil mining industry with a refinery, owned by the Shell Trinidad Ltd. at Port Fortin. The famous 95-acre Pitch Lake, the asphalt lake from which Raleigh used to caulk his ships in 1595, is situated in the ward of La Brea and is one of the greatest natural curiosities in the world. Agricultural products include some cocoa, coffee and coconuts.

The limbo, a West African tribal dance that was brought to Trinidad by slaves, is expertly performed in night clubs and hotels in Trinidad and Tobago. The dance is now a popular tourist attraction in many other Caribbean Islands.

Tall coconut trees cast their shadows across a beach area in Tobago as a small fishing boat puts out to sea.

TOBAGO is divided into seven parishes, St. David, St. Patrick, St. Andrew, St. George, St. Mary, St. Paul and St. John. There are also the islands of Little Tobago, Goat, Queen's and St. Giles or Melville. Chief crops include cocoa, coconuts, citrus, bananas and ground provisions. Tobago is also becoming better known as the focal point of the tourist industry of both islands.

A young marcher joins a contingent of Trinidad's police force on parade.